HAL LEONARD

BAGPIPE TUNE BOOK

BY RON BOWEN AND SARAJANE TRIER

ISBN 978-1-4950-2790-1

Contact us:
Hal Leonard
7777 West Bluemound Road
Milwaukee, WI 53213
Email: info@halleonard.com

In Europe, contact:
Hal Leonard Europe Limited
42 Wigmore Street
Marylebone, London, W1U 2RN
Email: info@halleonardeurope.com

In Australia, contact:
Hal Leonard Australia Pty. Ltd.
4 Lentara Court
Cheltenham, Victoria, 3192 Australia
Email: info@halleonard.com.au

CONTENTS

INTRODUCTION

Ron Bowen:

I was initially exposed to the Great Highland Bagpipe and its music through my father's participation in The Bridgeport Pipe Band in the mid-1950s (Bridgeport CT. USA). One Christmas, brother Will and I found child-size practice chanters under the tree. Lessons were torture. At age six, I found reading staff notation too difficult and learned my first tunes by ear. I was a very good mimic. Circumstances changed a short while later and I would not pick up another practice chanter until I was almost twenty-one. This time I was ready. One year later, in September 1973, Will and I both joined the Grade 1 Waterloo Regional Police Pipe Band.

This story is far from typical and would not have occurred had circumstances been different. We were surrounded by a multitude of talented pipers and outstanding pipe bands. We were hungry to learn, and many were generous with their time and talent. PM Alex Robertson in Woodstock, who was a legendary teacher and leader, gave me sage advice. "Ringo, you can learn something from the worst piper by listening to what he's doing incorrectly and avoiding those shortcomings."

Over the following decades I played in several top Grade 1 and Grade 2 bands. I taught constantly and I built very successful programs along the way. My evolving experiences impacted my perspective greatly. I came to realize that unless you begin this journey at a very early age, you are not likely to reach the elevated performance levels of competition pipers (Open Solo or Grade 1 and 2 band pipers). Accordingly, I developed specific non-conforming theories and methodology for "The Average Piper." What or who is The Average Piper? Sarajane's story, below, resonates.

Sarajane Trier:

The highland bagpipe was not my primary instrument. I was a flute major and through years of hard work and advanced musical education I became proficient at many instruments. I "discovered" the Highland Bagpipe and its music at a Master Class in college. Everything seemed wrong. The instrument was complicated and seemingly unsophisticated. The dramatic and subtle differences in its music was confusing to me. Still, inexplicably, I was drawn. I put it on my bucket list.

At age forty I began learning the bagpipe. I was surprised at how little my formal education and musical proficiency had prepared me for this experience. At times it seemed to be a handicap. Even more frustrating was the lack of appropriate resources. For people who were not associated with the music through family or culture, there was very little at a beginner or even intermediate level that was readily available. I had an instructor and a lesson book, however there were only a few tunes, and they went from rather easy to incredibly difficult in just a few pages.

Ron Bowen:

These words hit like a hammer on an anvil. Without strong cultural ties and an early association, many are destined for a life-long experience of frustration. The instrument, although logical, is extremely complicated and a major source of frustration for many. Equally so is its music. Most of the music, both historically and in more recent times, is composed by exceptional pipers for exceptional pipers. There is limited material that lies within the abilities of The Average Piper.

Teaching both young and mature individuals and building bands brought this reality into acute focus. Out of need, I started composing tunes that I felt were appropriate for those who may have started later in life, without the mechanical dexterity of someone pre-teen or in their early teens. In 2006 I built a highly successful program at a military school and found my methods and tune selections accelerated learning and proficiency without negatively impacting those with greater ambition.

Sarajane Trier:

I researched other instructional materials and found pretty much the same everywhere. There was significant emphasis placed on embellishments before the learner was vaulted into seemingly impossible tunes. The lack of level-appropriate tune books made understanding the unique musical concepts difficult. Learning was slow and unpleasant. Everything I could find was well beyond my ability and worse yet, I had no idea how the music should sound. Although I am a very good sight-reader, I had few points of reference with bagpipe music. I found it greatly different from my formal training. I had lots of questions. What are the nuances of the phrasing? Where do the embellishments land relevant to the beat? And then for the absolute strangest question-how long is a dot, because it wasn't lining up with the musical math I had learned.

My life changed while attending my first summer workshop. I found that top-notch instructors from around the world were real people and incredibly willing to answer all these questions. They were beginning to see their own music through a slightly different lens. Through hours of conversation, we were able to create relevant connections between bagpipe music and traditional music theory. Everything became incredibly clear, and, over time, my playing improved significantly. Still there was a lack of material within my growing abilities and it seemed that every new music book I purchased contained but one or two tunes that I could get my hands around.

The instructional approach to our first book, *The Hal Leonard Bagpipe Method*, is the tangible result of many hours of collaboration (arguments) with Ron (Ringo). He was the newly appointed bagpipe instructor at St. John's Northwestern Military Academy and was also helping several bands and individuals in southern Wisconsin. Ringo had been playing bagpipes, as his only instrument, since 1971 and had achieved success with several excellent bands in Ontario. With the school, his challenge was to advance young boys onto the pipes and playing tunes for parades and performances within an incredibly short period of time (roughly ten weeks). With the bands and adults in the area, he was challenged to expand their repertoires beyond the few tunes that everyone seemed to play. In 2009 I joined Ringo as an instructor, and we further refined our teaching methods.

Through long periods of discussion and through trial and error we discovered critical "missing links" between bagpipe teaching methods and the way other musicians are taught. Following long hours of research, discussions with other accomplished pipers, and testing ideas, we created *The Hal Leonard Bagpipe Method*.

The music of the Highland Bagpipe is most often performed without sheet music as a guide. In learning new tunes, I found that hearing the melody of the tune first was incredibly helpful. I would play a recording in a loop until I could sing it. (I did this while driving, cooking, cleaning - you name it!) I could also play my practice chanter with the sound file, at first with the printed music, and then eventually without.

You will find both traditional and original compositions in this collection, most of which will fall within the abilities of The Average Piper. Many of the traditional tunes began as folk songs, handed down from generation to generation. At some point they were repurposed for the fiddle and the bagpipe and started their lives anew. Over the years there has been some success in standardizing the settings however multiple variations can still be found today, some complicated and some less so. You may also encounter extended versions, harmonies, and countermelodies, all intended to add variety and additional interest for the audience. As in all musical idioms, the staff notation is a guide. The musician must bring forward the emotion and feeling within the music.

The essence of the music is within the melody. Embellishments are intended to enhance the melody however, they should not be played to the detriment of the melody, technique, timing, or tempo. As your abilities allow, embellishments should be included to the highest degree possible without doing damage to the aforementioned. There are some who disagree with this philosophy, and I accept that point of view, however nothing causes me (or your audience) more displeasure than to hear a beautiful melody compromised for the sake of embellishments. The equal can be said of a bad sounding instrument. My basic rule is to play within your abilities, both in the selection of your music and in the inclusion of embellishments.

We hope that you find these words and the tunes within this book helpful. Please don't hesitate to reach out to either of us at **www.thebagpipeplace.com**.

–Ringo & Sarajane

ALL THE BLUE BONNETS
ARE OVER THE BORDER

Traditional

March

AMAZING GRACE

Traditional

THE AULD HOOSE

Traditional

ASPEN BANK

Traditional

AULD LANG SYNE

Traditional

AVA'S JIG

By Ron Bowen

AVA'S SONG

By Ron Bowen

BANJO BOB

By Ron Bowen

THE BATTLECREEK REEL

By Ron Bowen

BECAUSE HE WAS A BONNIE LAD

Traditional

BILL SAWYER

By Ron Bowen

BLACK VELVET BAND

Traditional

Air

THE BLUE BELLS OF SCOTLAND

Traditional

March

THE BLUE DUCK

By Ron Bowen

THE BONNIE BLUE FLAG

Copyright © 2021 by HAL LEONARD LLC

Traditional

BONNIE DUNDEE

Copyright © 2021 by HAL LEONARD LLC

Traditional

BONNIE GALLOWAY

Traditional

THE BOYS OF ST. JOHN'S

By Ron Bowen

THE BONNIE LASS O' FYVIE

Traditional

THE BROWN HAIRED MAIDEN

Traditional

BUGLE HORN

Traditional

CLARA'S JIG

By Ron Bowen

CELTIC NATIONS PIPE BAND

By Ron Bowen

March

THE CHICK 'N BUG

By Ron Bowen

(Harmonies 2nd time through last part)

COCK O' THE NORTH

Traditional

March

COCK OF THE ROOST

Traditional

COLLIN'S CATTLE

Traditional

COLONEL MacLEOD

Traditional

Reel

THE CROOKED PATH

By Ron Bowen

DRUM MAJOR SERGIO GIL

By Ron Bowen

THE DALTON

By Ron Bowen

March

DANNY BOY

Traditional

Londonderry Air

THE DAWNING OF THE DAY

Traditional

March

DRUM MAJOR OX GARA

By Ron Bowen

March

THE FAIRY DANCE

Traditional

Reel

EMMA CATHARINE

By Ron Bowen

March

THE FLOWERS OF THE FOREST

Traditional

Slow March

GLEN ELLYN

By Ron Bowen

Strathspey

THE 42ND BLACK WATCH

Traditional

THE FOX AND THE HEN

By Ron Bowen

GARRY OWEN

Traditional

THE GHOST OF HOLT HOUSE

By Ron Bowen

March

GOING HOME

Traditional

Slow March

THE GREEN HILLS OF TYROL

Traditional

Retreat

THE HIGHLAND CRADLE SONG

Traditional

GREENSLEEVES

Traditional

THE GROUSE'S CLAW

By Ron Bowen

HIGHLAND LADDIE

Traditional

A HUNDRED PIPERS

Traditional

HUMOURS OF WHISKEY

Traditional

JENNY'S BAWBEE

Traditional

I'M A DOUN FOR LACK O' JOHNNIE

Traditional

JOCK WILSON'S BALL

Traditional

JACK DUNBAR

By Ron Bowen

JILL SWINFORD OF WEST ALLIS

By Ron Bowen

THE JUNKMAN'S TUNE

By Ron Bowen

THE JOLLY MAIDEN

By Ron Bowen

LADY MACKENZIE OF FAIRBURN

Traditional

JOHN MITCHELL'S JIG

By Ron Bowen

KATHLEEN COBB

By Ron Bowen

THE KEEL ROW

Traditional

Strathspey

LT. MARK WEIGEL

By Ron Bowen

March

KELLY - THE BOY FROM KILLANE

Traditional

March

LET ERIN REMEMBER THE DAYS OF OLD

Traditional

March

LORD LOVAT'S LAMENT

Traditional

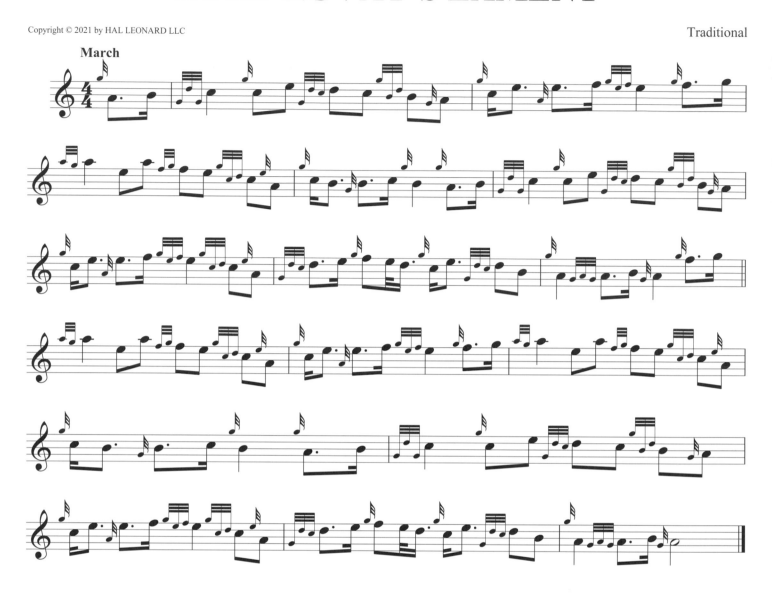

MAID OF THE GLEN

By Ron Bowen

THE MAIDS OF THE BLACK GLEN

Traditional

Strathspey

LORD DUNMORE'S JIG

Traditional

Jig

MacCRIMMON WILL NEVER RETURN

Traditional

Slow Air

A MAN'S A MAN FOR A' THAT

Traditional

MARCHE DU PETRE

Traditional

THE MILWAUKEE FIRE
& POLICE PIPE BAND

By Ron Bowen

THE MINSTREL BOY

Traditional

MISS GIRDLE

Copyright © 2021 by HAL LEONARD LLC

Traditional

Reel

MIST COVERED MOUNTAINS OF HOME

Copyright © 2021 by HAL LEONARD LLC

Traditional

Slow March

MOLLY MALONE

Traditional

Lullaby

Chorus

MY HOME

Traditional

Slow March

THE MOUSE'S TRAIL

By Ron Bowen

MY LODGING'S ON THE COLD GROUND

Traditional

MY LOVE SHE'S BUT A LASSIE YET

Traditional

March

NASHOTAH ROAD

By Ron Bowen

March

NAGAWICKA ROAD

By Ron Bowen

March

NIAGARA MIST

By Ron Bowen

Slow Air

NEIL FLINT'S JIG

By Ron Bowen

THE ORANGE AND BLUE

Traditional

O'ER THE WATER TO CHARLIE

Traditional

THE OLD RUSTIC GATE

By Ron Bowen

March

OLD TOM'S EYE

By Ron Bowen

March

OLIVIA

By Ron Bowen

March

PADDY'S GREEN SHAMROCK SHORES

Traditional

Slow Air

PADDY'S LEATHER BREECHES

Traditional

PETER A. STANFORD

By Ron Bowen

THE PIKEMAN'S MARCH

Traditional

THE PIOBAIREACHD OF DONALD DHU

Traditional

PM ZACH MAUER

By Ron Bowen

THE PIPER OF DRUMMOND

Traditional

RETURN TO ST. CATHARINES

By Ron Bowen

THE ROAD TO MONEYREAGH

By Ron Bowen

March

RAGNAR'S MARCH

By Ron Bowen

THE ROAD TO THE ISLES

Traditional

Slow March

THE ROCK INN

By Ron Bowen

SCOTLAND THE BRAVE

Traditional

SANDY'S WEE DRUMMERS

By Ron Bowen

ROBIN ADAIR

Traditional

March

THE ROWAN TREE

Traditional

March

SCOTS WA HAE WI' WALLACE BLED

Traditional

SEAN SOUTH OF GARRY OWEN

Traditional

SJNMA HORNPIPE

By Ron Bowen

Hornpipe

SOMETHING DIFFERENT

By Ron Bowen

Horn-Reel

STAR OF COUNTY DOWN

Traditional

March

STEAMBOAT

Traditional

TOM DALTON'S JIG

By Ron Bowen

TOWER MOUNTAIN ROAD

By Ron Bowen

THE TUCSON ROADRUNNER

By Ron Bowen

TUGAINN LEAMSA'S DEAN CABHAIG

Traditional

WELLS STREET TAVERN

By Ron Bowen

March

WE'RE NO AWA TAE BIDE AWA

Traditional

WHEN IRISH EYES ARE SMILING

Traditional

WALY WALY

Copyright © 2021 by HAL LEONARD LLC

Traditional

March or Slow Air

THE WEARING OF THE GREEN

Copyright © 2021 by HAL LEONARD LLC

Traditional

March

WHEN THE BATTLE'S O'ER

Traditional

THE WHIPPING POST

By Ron Bowen

WILL YE NO COME BACK AGAIN?

Traditional

THE WITCH'S TIT

By Ron Bowen

WINGS

Traditional

Learn to Play Today
with folk music instruction from Hal Leonard

Hal Leonard Bagpipe Method

The Hal Leonard Bagpipe Method is designed for anyone just learning to play the Great Highland bagpipes. This comprehensive and easy-to-use beginner's guide serves as an introduction to the bagpipe chanter. It includes access to online video lessons with demonstrations of all the examples in the book! Lessons include: the practice chanter, the Great Highland Bagpipe scale, bagpipe notation, proper technique, grace-noting, embellishments, playing and practice tips, traditional tunes, buying a bagpipe, and much more!
00102521 Book/Online Video $14.99

Hal Leonard Banjo Method – Second Edition

Authored by Mac Robertson, Robbie Clement & Will Schmid. This innovative method teaches 5-string, bluegrass style. The method consists of two instruction books and two cross-referenced supplement books that offer the beginner a carefully-paced and interest-keeping approach to the bluegrass style.
00699500 Book 1 Only..$9.99
00695101 Book 1 with Online Audio...............$17.99
00699502 Book 2 Only..$9.99
00696056 Book 2 with CD................................$17.99

Hal Leonard Brazilian Guitar Method

by Carlos Arana
This book uses popular Brazilian songs to teach you the basics of the Brazilian guitar style and technique. Learn to play in the styles of Joao Gilberto, Luiz Bonfá, Baden Powell, Dino Sete Cordas, Joao Basco, and many others! Includes 33 demonstration tracks.
00697415 Book/Online Audio $17.99

Hal Leonard Chinese Pipa Method

by Gao Hong
This easy-to-use book serves as an introduction to the Chinese pipa and its techniques. Lessons include: tuning • Western & Chinese notation basics • left and right hand techniques • positions • tremolo • bending • vibrato and overtones • classical pipa repertoire • popular Chinese folk tunes • and more!
00121398 Book/Online Video $19.99

Hal Leonard Dulcimer Method – Second Edition

by Neal Hellman
A beginning method for the Appalachian dulcimer with a unique new approach to solo melody and chord playing. Includes tuning, modes and many beautiful folk songs all demonstrated on the audio accompaniment. Music and tablature.
00699289 Book..$12.99
00697230 Book/Online Audio...........................$19.99

Hal Leonard Flamenco Guitar Method

by Hugh Burns
Traditional Spanish flamenco song forms and classical pieces are used to teach you the basics of the style and technique in this book. Lessons cover: strumming, picking and percussive techniques • arpeggios • improvisation • fingernail tips • capos • and much more. Includes flamenco history and a glossary.
00697363 Book/Online Audio $17.99

Hal Leonard Irish Bouzouki Method

by Roger Landes
This comprehensive method focuses on teaching the basics of the instrument as well as accompaniment techniques for a variety of Irish song forms. It covers: playing position • tuning • picking & strumming patterns • learning the fretboard • accompaniment styles • double jigs, slip jigs & reels • drones • counterpoint • arpeggios • playing with a capo • traditional Irish songs • and more.
00696348 Book/Online Audio $12.99

Hal Leonard Mandolin Method – Second Edition

Noted mandolinist and teacher Rich Del Grosso has authored this excellent mandolin method that features great playable tunes in several styles (bluegrass, country, folk, blues) in standard music notation and tablature. The audio features play-along duets.
00699296 Book..$10.99
00695102 Book/Online Audio...........................$16.99

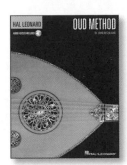

Hal Leonard Oud Method

by John Bilezikjian
This book teaches the fundamentals of standard Western music notation in the context of oud playing. It also covers: types of ouds, tuning the oud, playing position, how to string the oud, scales, chords, arpeggios, tremolo technique, studies and exercises, songs and rhythms from Armenia and the Middle East, and 25 audio tracks for demonstration and play along.
00695836 Book/Online Audio $14.99

Hal Leonard Sitar Method

by Josh Feinberg
This beginner's guide serves as an introduction to sitar and its technique, as well as the practice, theory, and history of raga music. Lessons include: tuning • postures • right- and left-hand technique • Indian notation • raga forms; melodic patterns • bending strings • hammer-ons, pull-offs, and slides • changing strings • and more!
00696613 Book/Online Audio $16.99
00198245 Book/Online Media $19.99

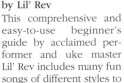

Hal Leonard Ukulele Method

by Lil' Rev
This comprehensive and easy-to-use beginner's guide by acclaimed performer and uke master Lil' Rev includes many fun songs of different styles to learn and play. Includes: types of ukuleles, tuning, music reading, melody playing, chords, strumming, scales, tremolo, music notation and tablature, a variety of music styles, ukulele history and much more.
00695847 Book 1 Only.......................................$7.99
00695832 Book 1 with Online Audio...............$12.99
00695948 Book 2 Only.......................................$7.99
00695949 Book 2 with Online Audio...............$11.99